Praise for *Mindfulness and the Art of Choice*

"This is a wonderful little book, and I feel privileged to have had the honor of editing it for Loving Healing Press. In clear, easy-to-follow language, in a very well organized manner, she guides people from suffering to living, by the use of exercises that are based on thousands of years of wisdom and a great deal of modern research. I thoroughly recommend this book."　　　—Robert Rich, PHD, author
Cancer: A Personal Challenge
Here are the 2 testimonials:

"We have little control over so many aspects of our lives, but we *can* control how we *interpret* what happens to us, and we can learn to interpret almost any stressful event in a neutral or even a positive way. If you're carrying any hurt from your past, Dr. Sherman's book will give you the power you need to banish that hurt forever."
—Robert Epstein, Ph.D., Host of "Psyched!" on Sirius
Former Editor-in-Chief, *Psychology Today*

"Karen Sherman presents to the reader simple, yet profound ways to help people get "unstuck" from many of life's daily issues. Through sharing her personal experiences and those of clients she guides the reader toward mastering The Art of Choice."
—Stephan Rechtschaffen, M.D., cofounder of OMEGA.
Author of *Timeshifting: Creating More Time to Enjoy Your Life* and coauthor of *Vitality and Wellness*.

MINDFULNESS AND THE ART OF CHOICE:

TRANSFORM YOUR LIFE

KAREN H. SHERMAN, PH.D.

Library of Congress Cataloging-in-Publication Data

Sherman, Karen, 1948-
   Mindfulness and the art of choice : transform your life / Karen H. Sherman.
        p. cm.
   Includes bibliographical references and index.
   ISBN-13: 978-1-932690-51-4 (trade paper : alk. paper)
   ISBN-10: 1-932690-51-4 (trade paper : alk. paper)
   1. Self-esteem. 2. Self-help techniques. 3. Choice (Psychology) I. Title.
   BF697.5.S46S54 2008
   158--dc22

                                    2007051746

Distributed by: Baker & Taylor, Ingram Book Group
Published by:
Loving Healing Press
5145 Pontiac Trail
Ann Arbor, MI 48105

http://www.LovingHealing.com or
info@LovingHealing.com
Fax +1 734 663 6861

To Judy who stood by me through it all
and to Rich who kept believing in me.

Table of Contents

Exercises in this Book

Preface

After having been raised in a home that was dysfunctional beyond imagination, I felt as if the drama in my life would take me under like a merciless tidal wave. There I was, a grown adult with a successful career that included my own private practice, yet I was drowning in despair. Growing up in a horribly dysfunctional family had turned me into an overactive and dissatisfied individual. I was rarely happy about the results of most of my choices.

Somehow, through it all, I was able to be very successful when it came to my career. I had managed to build a private practice and was teaching college courses in Psychology. But my private life was a whole other story. Most of the time, I felt out of control, often barely squeaking past or around struggles. The pivotal moment for me came after a long bout with depression. At times, the pain was unbearable and I wasn't sure if I could withstand it.

But rather than topple from it, I chose to face my problems and take charge of creating a life that would be mine. I decided to stop being a slave to my past history, but to have a life that was meaningful and satisfying to me. Out of this journey of recovery and reclaiming my life, I developed *The Art of Choice.*

As I reflected on the experiences I went through, as devastating and painful as they were, I came to believe they had two purposes. In addition to building my own inner strength, I truly feel that the knowledge I have gained was meant for me to share with others. I invite you try the same Exercises and tools that have had profound, life-altering results for many of my clients. In doing so, I am confident that you will gain your *own* inner power as you create a sense of what is important and meaningful in your life.

Each of you is entitled to have "the good life." Most of you don't experience this, because you're so caught up in *reacting,* continually recycling old patterns that keep you stuck and emotionally frozen. But, by practicing the simple tools that I used to free myself, and will share with you in *The Art of Choice,* you'll learn how to live *mindfully* and create the great life you want.

Introduction

I chose the term, *The Art of Choice*, to differentiate it from the world of science. Science is exact and precise. Art involves the abstract and the creative. It is not definitive; rather it is open and it can flow to unusual potentials and possibilities.

I also recognized that my clients needed a sense of how "to do" the world. They wanted to know how to handle the different things in their lives. They wanted to feel a sense of readiness, security, and being in control.

If there were but one way to handle things, there might be a feeling of comfort, a way to know what is right or wrong. But it would soon become boring. Since you are all different people with different experiences, needs, and backgrounds, there is no one solution that fits all. More importantly, there is no way to anticipate every situation that might occur.

There is, I discovered, a way to approach life so that you feel a sense of being prepared, of being ready, of being grounded. This self-confident approach is generated from within. It comes from being in touch, being connected with yourself. Through this self-awareness, you will be able to deal with whatever comes your way.

Sometimes it seems as if there's just too much going on in your life. As a shortcut, you will use whatever you know to get by. And what you know is usually a mere repetition of what you learned to do in the past. Sometimes you don't even realize that you are doing this. The reaction is fast and automatic. The response you have is the consequence of being emotionally frozen—it goes on without your awareness. If you try to respond to each situation automatically, as you did in the past, you end up in a constant state of reacting.

But when you observe yourself—your thoughts, feelings, sensations, and behaviors—you have an opening in which to step out of your reactive nature (or mindlessness). It is then that *The Art of Choice* becomes available to you. You can consider that different options exist, instead of seeing and accepting those things you have done in the past. They are not the only choice. You stay open to various new possibilities rather than anticipate a prescribed ending. You make choices that reflect your needs, in the present, rather than putting into motion old survival patterns to try to please others. You can stay open to observing the consequences of your choices and develop the ability to flow and to adapt accordingly, letting go when necessary.

When you make a conscious choice, it is from a true connection to, and trust in, yourself. Your approach will come from love rather than fear. You'll embrace an exploratory and playful attitude as an art. It is from this vantage point that you will be able to clearly access all that is available to you to create a life for yourself that is full and satisfying.

Rather than being an exact equation, *The Art of Choice* is a creative approach. Rather than looking for a consequence, *The Art of Choice* will teach you how to adopt an imaginative way to move through life by being in a process that is always "at choice."

PART I:

HOW THE ART OF CHOICE WORKS

1

The Universal Problem:
The World's a Crazy Place to Live in

Not so long ago, pop music performer Britney Spears got married and divorced in a little over a 2-day period. A married Palestinian woman with two young children left them behind to become a suicide bomber, killing four Israelis. Almost every week, all over the U.S., infants are found on the steps of a church or, even worse, in dumpsters. And occasionally, in New York subways, people push other people into oncoming trains for no discernible reason.

Open any newspaper on any given day and you'll have clear evidence that the world is apparently going crazy! Is it a "sign of the times?" No, not really. In times past, a kind, loving man was nailed to a cross. A brave woman in France was burned at the stake. Millions of innocent people were put to death in Germany because one man decided they deserved to be. Hundreds of zealous followers agreed to commit suicide in Jonestown at the suggestion of their leader. And some people starve themselves in order to look beautiful while others die because they are starving. The world has always been a little "crazy." It's only the situations at particular points in history that vary.

Unfortunately, many of you obsess over these matters, take them to heart and end up with feelings of anxiety, uncertainty, and fear. Others of you do not feel a personal connection to these world dramas and are able to accept that they go on, have always gone on, and will continue to go on and on.

Even if the worldly catastrophes do not grab you, it's easy to get caught up in the craziness of your personal world, causing tension to build. Why didn't your cousin invite your children to the wedding? The nerve of that other driver taking the spot you were waiting for! You keep having trouble with relationships because your father was an alcoholic. Your parents couldn't afford to send you to a more prestigious college, so now your employment opportunities are severely limited. Your sister's son has gotten involved with the wrong crowd. The guy you've gone out with for five years refuses to make a marriage commitment. Your parents' health is failing, but they refuse to get some form of assistance. You helped out a relative who was in financial distress, only to later find out he was short of money due to a gambling addiction.

The examples are endless. Stack a group of them up in close succession and you're really vulnerable to all the negative impacts of too much stress. At the very least, your world is not free, your world is not calm—there's just too much happening you can't control.

It is true that many uncontrollable things keep happening. No doubt, there will always be situations with which to contend—some are bumps, others feel more like a tornado. These are all part of life. The acceptance of that fact, alone, is very important because if you try to control everything or, at least, be prepared for everything, you will always feel out of control.

What is perhaps even more frustrating than not being able to change a situation is the additional fact that you cannot change another person. You can't make your parents more generous. You can't insist your friends include you in on a dinner plan. You can't get your significant others to stay on their diet. If you continue to expect or hope that a situation will change, or another person will somehow become what you would like them to be, it will only lead you to feel disappointment, anger, or perhaps a sense of helplessness. Your personal world then becomes a stage for drama.

So, does this mean you have to resign yourself to the "same old, same old?" Do you just have to accept that you're going to be bumped and bounced through your day-to-day existence, and hope the resulting damage won't be too overwhelming?

No! Because there is one thing over which you always have control. That one thing is your *reaction*. You can learn a process, which I have termed *The Art of Choice*, that will allow you to be "at choice" as a lifestyle. In doing so, not only will you get off the frenzied *merry-go-round*, you can also create a life that hums with richness and harmony.

2 The Personal Problem: Living a Life that's on "Auto-Pilot"

The world is quite different today from what it was in historical times. Perhaps the most significant difference is how technological we have all become. You can now visit all parts of the world. Perhaps one day you will all be making trips to the moon. You have the ability to stay current, and in a matter of moments, you can know what's going on throughout the world.

Your life has the benefits of ease and access—with potential for greater relaxation and free time. However, despite having all these benefits, our technology can also work against you. Suddenly, your life seems more harried, hectic and frantic, filled with too many things to get done.

With your lifestyle being so demanding, it's often hard to differentiate the cause from the effect, to tell which is the trigger and which is the result. Does the life you lead create a daily existence that seems to run on "auto-pilot"—or do you allow such an existence to be maintained because you are not even aware that it is happening? Most of you have come to accept the concept of needing to deal with "the cards that have been dealt to you." You have come to accept the idea of getting through life rather than *creating* your lives.

So why is it that most people function in this robotic way? Why do you remain in a state of auto-pilot? Because to go against these concepts means making a change. Change is, at the very least, discomforting. For some, making changes is downright frightening. When you continue to do the things you've always done, even if they don't bring the greatest amount of satisfaction or pleasure, there is one major benefit. That benefit is comfort.

Because this is what you've always done, you know how to do it.

A byproduct of living life this way is a state of mindlessness—you don't have to think about it. There are many everyday examples of acting mindlessly. If you're a good cook, you can make scrambled eggs for breakfast without really thinking about it. If you've driven to your friend's house on a regular basis, the next time you get in your car to go there, you arrive never really paying attention to the actual drive. Perhaps these are matters of convenience. But mindlessness also extends to every aspect of our daily living. Many people can eat an entire meal without really tasting it. Or you listen to your kids as they share the events that occurred in school that day, but you have not really heard what they've said. When you're involved in a relationship with a significant other, or a family member, or a work colleague, numerous conflicts or difficulties can arise that are the result of automatic reactions. You don't feel heard, you don't feel understood, and/or you don't feel loved. You get disappointed or hurt or angry.

Another benefit of not making changes is that you feel like you are in control—you know the outcome. Your risk factor is minimized. Furthermore, functioning in this manner releases you from your responsibility. If you're not all you can be, you can easily blame it on your past—something that happened to you, or something you didn't get. If you're out of sorts, it's because of all the horrible things that occurred that month, that week, or that day. As a psychologist who has spent years helping people heal from their wounds, I have heard countless people excuse themselves for the unhappy lives they have by saying, "I can't help it, that's how I feel."

Earlier, I mentioned my abominable formative years. Was my early life the worst environment ever? No. Unfortunately, I've had a few clients whose childhood stories were a lot worse. But my family still scored high on the dysfunctional scale.

I was exposed to almost every type of abuse there is. Though I wasn't subjected to physical abuse directly, I had to witness it over and over. My father would throw things or hit my mother. One time, my mother, sister, and I were preparing to leave our apartment. I don't remember why my father got angry, but what I vividly recall is that he grabbed her purse and flung it with all his might at her head. To this day, I'm still sickened by the image of her slumping to the floor as he connected with his target.

When my dad wasn't throwing things, he was raging at one of us. The littlest things set him off. But what triggered him one time would not upset him at another. I lived in total confusion. There was never any way to predict how to behave in order to avoid his wrath. The phone would ring in the middle of the afternoon during his nap— I'd run and try to grab it, but the first ring woke him up and all hell broke loose! The next time he napped, I disconnected the phone. When he woke up and found the phone off the hook, he went ballistic again. How do you please someone like that?

When I was eight, my younger sister was in a highchair in the kitchen and I was told to watch her. My parents were in the bedroom of our three-room apartment. All of a sudden I heard my mom screaming and I instantly knew my dad was about to punch her with his fists. I stood in the hallway, paralyzed—whose safety should I be more concerned about? If I went to protect my mother, my sister could fall out of the highchair. If I stayed to watch my baby sister, my mother could get brutalized.

As a psychologist, my specialty is in relationships. When people ask how long I have been doing this, I reply, "Since I was eight." And I'm not joking! My father had a string of affairs and I was always trying to salvage my parents' relationship. Strangely, they would sometimes come to me for help—or they found a way to put me in the middle. In that same kitchen where I watched my baby sister in the highchair, my parents had an awful fight about his latest fling—her name was June. I stood between the two of them, begging for them to stop yelling. Finally, I cried, "I'll call June and tell her to stop!" But this time the fight continued, my mother ended up with a black eye and she actually threw my father out that night. The weird thing is, even though I knew she was right, there was a part of me that didn't want my daddy to go. And when I missed his call because I went out to have a good time with my friend's family for the day, I was heartbroken. They never thought to have him call me back... it took me years to realize that often I was afraid to "miss out on things" because of this incident.

As inappropriate as it was, the responsibility for helping my parents was a role I was thrown into more times than I care to remember. I had a second sister who died just short of a month old. I did everything I could think of to soothe them. However, my parents were not able to contain their emotions even for the sake of their other two children. The drama was awful: terrible wailing, banging their heads on the crib. What was totally lacking in my parents was a concern for helping my sister and me deal with our emotions as well, or comprehending such a frightening and confusing event.

The inappropriateness of my parents' behavior was not limited to times when they were in horribly traumatic situations. I've said that I was a victim of almost every type of abuse—that included sexual. Most people, when they hear that term, conjure up visions of rape or molestation. But there are other types of behaviors that also cross boundaries and leave a child feeling unsafe, confused and violated. When I was a preadolescent, my father would bring me to lie in bed with him and cuddle me. My mother simply turned her back to this. At first, I didn't know how wrong this behavior was. It felt nice to lie up against him—like we had a special secret from my mother. It started to become discomforting as I got a little older. At my mother's urging, I accompanied him as he did his chores. As we drove in the car, he'd put his hand on my knee. If I objected, he'd make some remark as if there was something wrong with me. It became especially uncomfortable when he'd kiss me in the ear. By then I knew it was wrong. But when I stiffened up and didn't respond, he told me I'd never find a husband if I didn't stop being frigid.

"Where was your mother in all of this?" you might ask. Well, from what I now know as a therapist, she had the personality that was typical of a mother of a sexually abused daughter. She was neglectful and closed off. For me, of all the types of abuse I was subjected to, neglect landed the hardest. My mother worked during a time in history when most mothers didn't work. Consequently, she never came to class parties, she wasn't there on open school days, she was never home to help with homework. I was so envious of all the other kids. When I was really young, my grandmother would have to come to the class parties. Even though I loved my grandmother, I hated that she came—I was embarrassed because she was so much older than the other moms. (Today, when I think back, I feel badly about that—she actually was my saving grace.)

There were many nights when I waited to eat dinner with my parents. They'd call and say they were leaving their office and they were bringing home a pizza. I was so excited and couldn't wait to see them! But as it usually turned out, they got home so late that I'd fallen asleep— without dinner. The sad thing was, the hours my parents spent at work were for their own business, and so the demanding hours were of their own making.

When the neglect became too much to bear and I finally complained, guess how my mother responded? She'd stop talking to me. And when she *was* talking to me, it was frequently to offer criticism. My mother would often comment on my legs. She'd feign surprise that she had such lovely legs but mine were so unshapely. Apparently, my mom thought she was offering motherly advice—like the time she took me aside and said that I was the kind of woman who would have to wake up before my husband and put makeup on so he would find me attractive.

Add to all that, they were also horribly strict and never seemed to care about how out of place their rules made me feel in relation to my friends. For one of the school's boy/girl parties, all the girls were given permission to wear lipstick. My mother not only forbade me to wear it, I wasn't allowed to go unless she was assured the other girls were forbidden to wear it as well. My parents would give me a curfew before the end of a dance, then refuse to pick me up at that hour. In order to go, I'd have to find another strict parent who was picking up their child early and was also willing to drive me home. And for good measure, my father would frequently pick a fight with me right before I went out, making it almost impossible for me to enjoy myself after that.

As a young adult, my self-esteem was low and a sense of worthlessness predominated my life. I compensated in lots of ways in response to these feelings. Among them were always trying to please people, a constant weight problem as I attempted to nurture myself through food, living in constant drama, getting involved in relationships that reflected the same early childhood patterns. My feelings were intense—I was angry, I was depressed, and with a childhood like I had, who could blame me?

CVS/pharmacy

for all the ways you care℠

MS MEAGAN PALAKOWSKI

$5 off Purchase of $25 or More
(up to $5.00 value)
Expires 03/02/2009

49529374

ExtraCare Card #: *******3819

EXTRACARE CARD MUST BE PRESENTED TO
GET THESE SAVINGS. EXCLUDES
PRESCRIPTIONS, ALCOHOL, GIFT CARDS,
MONEY ORDERS, POSTAGE
LOTTERY AND TOBACCO
CARDS AND TOBACCO
BACK. TAX CHARGED
REQUIRED.

But I was strong. I was a survivor. In spite of it all, I got married, had two children and established a successful career. Was my life okay? Sure. But deep down, I wasn't truly happy within myself. As I worked to deal with my issues, the depression got worse. It was so bad that at one point that I wasn't sure I could take the pain.

It was that experience that helped snap me out of my mindlessness. I chose to live! I embarked on learning how to create a life that would bring me satisfaction and joy. I no longer allowed myself to merely react to whatever was presented to me. I set out to create the life I wanted as opposed to one that was a consequence of my past. I refused to accept that the unhappy circumstances of my upbringing would dictate how I lived my life. I was determined not to be held back by a past that dictated my future. The die had been cast but I made the conscious decision to break the mold.

It was from this point that I realized how the mindlessness of people takes place. When you're children, the only way you come to know your world is through experiencing it. You don't yet have the ability to think or understand things.

The most important people in your life are your parents—you are totally dependent on them. They're the ones with the goodies—they have the food, they have the shelter, and most importantly, they have the love to give. As children, you figure out what you have to do to get their love. When they're happy with you, you feel good. When they're displeased with you, you feel bad. Additionally, children are very egocentric as they grow up—they only see the world from their perspective. That's why when parents divorce, kids think it's something they did. Here's another example: when a younger sibling is born, the older child may have some normal jealousy and negative thoughts about the new "intruder." If the baby were to die, the older sib may believe it was his or her negative think-ing that caused it. Those situations and the accompany-ing feelings get wired into your bodily memory as a sur-vival mechanism to help you cope in the future–you don't have to relearn every experience.

But there is a downside to this survival shortcut. You come to view new experiences based on your past ones. That is, your past experiences act as filtering systems (negative influences on your way of thinking). New experi-ences are not being seen for what they have to offer as an opportunity to make a different choice.

To be concrete, and present a more typical example, let's say a mother asks why her son got a B+ rather than an A on a test. Let's even go further and say that the mother, in her own way, is trying to let the child know that she feels that he is very capable. The child, however, is likely to get the message that he didn't perform well enough and feel a sense of shame. Now, anytime this same child doesn't get an A, the same sense of shame comes into play and the child feels like a failure. With that kind of self-judgment, it's more than likely that his future academic attempts will be negatively impacted. With the filtering system in place, all other similar experiences will be experienced in the same way. To fine tune this sce-nario, let's say that this child generally does good work in a class but has trouble on a particular test. Even if a con-cerned teacher asks the child in a considerate way if there was some problem, the child may still hear the question as a criticism rather than as a concern. The reaction is an automatic one, again leaving the child feeling ashamed.

For most of you, your life is emotionally frozen because of your childhood filtering systems. You do not stop to consider that you are merely reacting through your behav-ior, in your thoughts, or with emotions that stem from your past. You do not have this awareness. Furthermore, you don't realize that the people who raised you were also living out the same process. In other words, the messages they sent you were the result of their limitations, not a true reflection of who you are.

When Daddy yells at you for spilling milk because he's had a tough day at work, you think you've done something wrong—or that something is wrong with you. You don't think Daddy's wrong. The bad feeling gets "wired in" and you carry that feeling into adulthood.

Additionally, negative experiences carry much more weight than positive ones. And since much of what you hold onto is negative, it leads to you becoming restricted as you address new situations. You use your energy to manage your internalized uncomfortable feelings. Most of you try to keep your reactions in check. In order to do this, you prevent yourselves from being in a present state that is open and free; you are, therefore, limiting yourselves in the ability to consider healthy questioning and creativity.

To become mindful, you have to realize how much of what you do is merely in the service of this damaging process. Only through this acknowledgement does one have the opportunity to change. You weren't bad children, and you aren't bad people because you spilled the milk. Now, here's the tricky part—to be truly free from the past you need to also be aware that your parents were merely playing out their mindlessness. I say it's tricky because it means you can't blame then. It means the responsibility for your life is in your hands.

But it also means that the power to have the life you want is *within* you. You can make the choice to connect with that inner power.

By all accounts, as an adult, I should have turned out to be a complete mess—and almost did, if not for the tools that became *The Art of Choice*. If I can turn all that around and end up well adjusted and happy, so can you.

<table>
<tr><td>

3

</td><td>

The Solution:

Read Our Bodies, Our Barometers

</td><td></td></tr>
</table>

Being human can be both a gift and a detriment. You have been blessed with a highly developed brain that gives you the ability to think things through, to problem solve. Unfortunately, most people have come to rely on their sensibilities so much that they have come to ignore or be unaware of their bodies. It's as if they are cut off at the neck and overly focused on understanding and analyzing.

Many emotions "talk" to you through your body. The sensations you get can act as wonderful barometers that let you know that there is something you are reacting to. But you lose vital information if you are cut off from your body and its signals. It's like when you get a fever—the fever is a mechanism to indicate there's something wrong that needs to be attended to. If you don't notice the fever, or if you simply ignore it, you are likely to get sicker, with a corresponding higher fever.

As another example, let me ask you what may seem like a bizarre question. How do you know when you have to go to the bathroom? It's not complicated—your body "feels" it. But if you're a little kid and you get involved in playing, you could very well not pick up the signal of your body, or not pay attention to it, and you would have an "accident."

Well, as an adult, if something triggers a strong feeling in you and you are not aware of a bodily reaction, or you do feel something but don't pay attention to it, you are likely to have an "accident," too. Your *accident* may come in a variety of forms—from shutting down to lashing out.

For example, I have worked with many clients with anger control problems who initially told me they have a short fuse. Through our work together, what they learn to do is to pay attention to their "bodily signals." When they recognize that their body is sending an anger signal, they can take action. They take this action *before* they get to the point where they feel out of control and behave in inappropriate ways. Their previous behavior was nothing more than mindless automatic reactions. By becoming aware of the signals in their body and paying attention to them, they have the opportunity to choose different options. They are no longer frozen in old habits, but gain awareness that opens the way for them to deal with uncomfortable situations in less destructive ways.

Though referring to people with tempers is an easy way to make this point, there are a lot of other behaviors that result from the same process of not being aware of your body.

I used to have a terrible fear of falling. So, when it was icy out, I'd get nervous that I would fall. My body would automatically tighten up from fear. Then, if I hit a patch of ice, my body was so tense that I went rigid and ended up exactly where I didn't want to be—toppling down.

One tragic example is when someone is driving and is struck by a drunk driver. Since the sober people realize that there is about to be an impending accident, they brace themselves, tightening up. The intoxicated driver often comes out of it with barely a scratch. Why? Because the liquor they have consumed makes them feel so loose, they flow with the impact. The more your tight, tense, and rigid your body is, the less flow and responsiveness you will have available. But, by no means am I advocating alcohol as a means to relax. Instead, here is a much better way to get relaxed and to start making positive changes:

Intro to Exercise #1

Because this is a book about choices, I am presenting you with two options for learning to relax. One option is to read the instructions and the exercise completely to get the overall concept and then practice it. Or, you can read the instructions into a tape recorder and play them back while you do the following exercise. If you choose the latter, read the instructions into the recorder slowly. This will enable you to have more time to complete the Exercise properly.

Before getting started, scan your body with your mind's eye. On a scale of 1-10, rate how tense you feel (with 10 being the most tense). Write this number down on a piece of paper. Two purposes are served when you learn to relax. The first objective is to help you become more sensitive to when you are tense, which is an indication that something's troubling you. Only when you respond to what's troubling you can you detach yourself from the emotion and be clearer and freer to make healthy choices. The second objective is that if you're already feeling tense, the mere practice of relaxing will help you feel better.

Exercise #1: Relaxing Your Body

1. Close your eyes. Put both feet flat on the ground and sit up fairly straight. Get comfortable.

2. Take in a long slow breath through your nose and bring it in past your throat, past your chest, and into your solar plexus — the area between your rib cage and navel. It's important you do this slowly. (Hint: pretend you are walking past a bakery and get a whiff of the delicious smells. Imagine how you would breathe in the aroma.)

3. Hold the breath for the count of three.

4. Now, let the breath out through a small opening in your lips – just as slowly. (Hint: Pretend that you are blowing at some lit candles but you're not trying to blow them out. You only want to make the flames flicker.)

5. Do this a second time. Slowly, bring your breath through your nostrils, past your throat, past your chest, into your solar plexus. Now hold for a count of 1, 2, 3—and release slowly through your lips, slowly, slowly.

6. After you've let out these two cleansing breaths, maintain a steady breathing pattern.

7. Still keeping your eyes closed, you're now going to do a series of tightenings and relaxings of various body parts. Place your attention on your toes. Tighten them up and hold. Now release them and wiggle them.

8. Move your attention to your calves. Again, tighten the muscles, hold, and release.

9. Move up to your thighs, tighten those muscles for a moment, then let go.

10. Now it's time to tighten your hips, buttocks, and stomach. Really tighten these areas for a few moments and then let go. Many people hold stress in their stomachs, so make sure you breathe into your stomach to loosen it up.

11. Move up to your chest and back, and do the same thing. This is also an area that holds a lot of tension. Tighten it up, hold, and relax. Don't forget to breathe slowly.

12. Now tighten up your arms and make fists with your hands. Let the tension out, shake your hands out.

13. Raise your shoulders up to your neck, and hold the muscles tight. Stress really gets held in this area. Okay, release and roll your shoulders out.

14. Finally, tighten up your face. Squeeze your eyelids and lips together. Hold and then loosen them up.

15. Still keeping your eyes closed, take a moment to scan your body once more. Notice if any part of your body feels tight. If it does, imagine carrying your breath to that part of the body and relax it.

16. Okay, open your eyes slowly.

On a scale of 1-10, with 10 being the most tense, how would you rate your degree of tightness now? Is the number less than it was before? Remember, this exercise serves you dually: it helps you become aware of your body and it helps you learn to relax. Use it as necessary when you feel yourself being too tense for comfort.

In order to start "hearing" your body, you have to "listen" to it in this manner. It may take a little time to get into the habit. Every day, at least one or two times a day, stop and tune into your body. It doesn't matter what time of day, where you are, or what you're doing. Take a moment and scan your body for tension. The more you learn to "listen" to your body, the more you will be able to pick up its signals.

This is an important step for being alert rather than simply going through the motions. This step is vital for learning to flow and becoming artful in living "in choice."

4	The Solution: Quieting the Noisy Mind	

As much as you have numbed yourself to the messages your body, you have also learned to ignore the constant chatter in your mind. More likely than not, at any given moment, you are entertaining some thought that you're not even aware of.

Imagine that you work in an office, and outside, city workers are doing some construction. At first, the noise is annoying and may even interfere with your concentration. But as the project goes on and on and on, you eventually get used to the noise. In fact, what you initially found so bothersome hardly registers any more. It's become part of the regular background noise that you hardly notice.

Starting to be aware of your thoughts is similar to becoming aware of your bodily sensations. All you need to do is to question yourself about what you're thinking. Chances are the thoughts are something negative about what someone did or didn't do, or about what someone said or didn't say. Because you're now aware of the thought, you can start to challenge it. Why is what the person said or did upsetting to you? Does it remind you of something else? Was there another time in your life when something similar happened and you felt hurt or insecure or afraid? Also, notice if your body is tensing up.

Or, perhaps, the thoughts are self-critical where you are making judgments about yourself. Who, in your past, said these kinds of things to you?

The attempt to let go of old thinking patterns and create new ones is like getting yourself out of being stuck in the snow with your car. The only way to get unstuck and moving again is to make a new path. You need to change the direction of the wheel. If you keep going back and forth in the track that is already there, you will merely dig yourself in deeper and deeper.

Once you become aware of the thoughts and what they represent, you can work with them. Taking the example of someone doing something that made you feel bad, are there any other possibilities to explain why that person may have acted as they did? Let's say you had a doctor's appointment and your friend didn't call to see how it went. If you expected them to call, or calling is something you would do, chances are you will be hurt or disappointed. Bear in mind that expectations are filtering systems and that's why you automatically got upset. ("Filtering system" means that what you are seeing is not necessarily accurate, but rather is colored by your own perception, and usually based on something that happened in your past.) Consider this: perhaps your friend was raised to believe that it's intrusive to call, and was respecting your privacy. Or, maybe they got a migraine and were too sick to call. Your expectations have set you up for the automatic emotional reaction you had and therefore, you weren't able to even consider any other possibilities. Starting to be aware of your thoughts, and their mindlessness, will allow you to challenge them.

What about those paralyzing self-judgments? Chances are they are "old tapes" that just keep replaying, waiting for you to push the stop button. I attended a self-help group years ago to stop smoking. Of the many tools they offered, one was the suggestion that when you became aware that you were thinking about a cigarette, you were to change the thought to *anything* else. I remembered this concept of only being able to think one thought at a time and applied it years later when I heard my father's voice in my head putting me down. I'd make myself aware of what I was thinking. Then, though it was hard at first, I'd replace it with *anything* else. It started out being difficult to do. At times, if it got really hard, I'd yell, "STOP!" Eventually, just like dutifully going to a gym makes it easier to lift the weights, I was able to catch the thoughts and turn them off much faster and with greater ease.

When it is very clear that you are only repeating what you heard your parents say and have come to accept that they, too, fell victim to mindlessness, you can merely refuse to run the same message. It's garbage—just throw it out.

These thoughts are very ingrained for some people. Merely becoming aware of them and their root may still not allow you to disengage from them. Should you find this to be the case, there is an exercise I use in therapy that has been extremely helpful to clients.

Exercise #2: Quieting the Noisy Mind

1. Allow yourself to imagine how old you were when you got the message(s) that have made you feel so bad; the one(s) that are the reason for all this negative thinking. Now, within your imagination picture both yourself as a child at that age, and yourself at the age you are now.

2. Let the child express what he/she is feeling to you as the adult. The child can communicate in whatever way is most comfortable—with words, with facial expressions, with body language, or even telepathically. The job of the "adult you" is to just listen—make no attempts at explanation or even understanding. Just experience unconditional love and total acceptance.

3. When the child part of you is done expressing the feelings, let the adult you go over to the child and express love. In your imagination, feel the connection and the love between the two parts.

4. This type of visualization can be very healing. The brain is capable of making new neural connections. Thus, by allowing the old feelings and thoughts to be expressed by the child part of you and received by the loving adult you, new experiences, new filtering systems are being created. If, after you do such work, there is still some hesitation on your part to make changes, let yourself know that it is okay to have these feelings. But make the choice to act in a way that is more fitting to your actual current situation—not according to what has happened in the past.

5. "But what if the messages ring true?" you may ask. Again, become aware of them. Then, chal-

lenge them and dispute them—are they truly accurate? If they're not, set them aside with the rest of the garbage. If there is some truth to them, you now have the opportunity, the choice, to take action to make a change. That change can be either within yourself or in the actions you take in regard to someone else. Either way, there's a clearing and that clearing opens you up to consider different alternatives. As an example, perhaps you have gotten the message that you aren't a caring enough person because you're never on time and that's disrespectful to others. You can take certain steps to ensure that you will be prompt in the future and perhaps even apologize for your past behavior.

The practice of meditation has become very popular in recent years. Basically, by focusing on one's breath or on a mantra, or a visual focal point, you learn to release your thoughts—to quiet the noise. For most of you, your thoughts come as quickly as a semi-automatic rapid firing gun. Thus, even as you try to give full attention to what you've chosen to focus on, the old thoughts come back over and over and over again. Therefore, it's quite easy to lose the focus.

When I began meditating, as a way to focus, I used to count from one to ten, and then start over at one again. One time, I realized I was up to 18. My focusing had become mindless. Rather than becoming annoyed, I just went back to one. When you realize you're no longer focused, the trick is to *let go* of the distracting thought rather than turning your focus to it, which totally removes you from meditating.

Aside from learning to quiet your distracting thoughts, I've found that meditating also allows you to learn to let them go. When you do not let go, you attach your attention to the damaging thoughts, thereby giving them more energy and further perpetuating them. In my experience, learning to let go is one of the greatest benefits of meditating. Once you have learned to let go, if you find yourself in a situation that upsets you, taking a slow deep breath with the intention of not holding onto the bothersome thought will allow you to release the energy from it.

Each time you release an old, damaging thought you will have made a choice. By taking this initial action, you are then mentally freer and open to being aware of other possibilities—you are living "in choice."

5	**Becoming Unfrozen**	

I see this process of getting in touch with oneself as similar to how one deals with a garden plagued by weeds. Some of you will just turn your attention away from the fact that the weeds are there. Most of you will attempt to deal with the weeds, trying to get rid of them. If there are only a few weeds, you only have a small problem and do not have to expend much effort. On the other hand, if the weeds are rampant, you have a big problem that requires a lot of your attention. So, you decide to put out the required effort to get rid of the weeds. You go in with clippers and cut them down, and the weeds are gone—but alas, only temporarily. The results are short-lived because you merely responded to the external situation. In order to really deal with the problem, it is necessary to get to what is underneath: the roots.

It is through the process of *non-reactivity* that you can truly get a better grasp of what you want, what is important to you, what feels right for your needs, what is truly meaningful, what is connected and authentic. Remember, most of your behavior is an automatic response to the past. It's likely that you have not been aware of the process, and therefore, have not been able to shed these behaviors. By constantly getting caught up in the things outside of you, your attention continues to be drawn outwardly. The weeds come back and again require attention. And since this is the way that most of you have lived your life, you are clueless about internal sense of self; about your internal experience—what is really important to you, if something feels good to you or not.

In the previous chapter, I talked about learning to become aware of your thoughts and letting go of the ones that are not valid and do not support you. After mastering this ability, I gained a much better self-image. I actually came to grips with the idea that I was worthy and deserved to be treated a certain way. Since I had become very committed to observing myself objectively, my next step was to be honest with myself. With all this work, was I in fact gaining the results I wanted? Sadly, I realized I was still emotionally frozen in the *actions* I took. So, even though I had grown in my awareness, my behavior was still a repetition of old patterns rather than actions that were really a reflection of what I wanted. And so, in effect, I was still a slave to negative reactions.

Not only are you often clueless about your own needs and wants, you also do not realize that there are actually choices in how you can act. *What you have always done is not the only possibility of what can be done.* Read the last sentence again. Yes, options, alternatives, choices are available to you!

It may be hard to consider that you have choices when you're experiencing a debilitating emotion, but it is true. And they are available to you! Even though everyone experiences similar emotions such as anger, sadness, or happiness, the *responses* to these emotions vary from person to person. Let's use experiencing anger as an example. Some people will shut down—they may stop talking, pull within themselves, or leave the situation entirely. Others will lash out. The outward expressions can also vary—some people will become physically destructive while others will respond verbally. I have known people who cry when they are angry. Clearly, there are numerous ways to react to an emotion. For any one individual, however, there is usually a consistent response to felt emotions. The consistent response is the one that has been learned early on in life and then has been maintained habitually. It is *not* one of choice. This brings you back to becoming aware of yourself and learning that there are possibilities other than what you have always done.

So many people complain that they are not happy in their life situation. Many people feel that life is about enduring; or, perhaps enduring with fleeting moments of happiness. Your overall attitude and behavior are the result of dealing with situations the best you can—which usually amounts to doing what you know, what you've always done. Then you get frustrated that nothing seems to change. One of the definitions of insanity is "doing the same thing over and over, but expecting the outcome to be different." Again, *there are other possibilities*, but they require taking a *different* action.

In some instances, people will come to realize that what they are doing is not really getting the preferred result. However, they are able to acknowledge that the result is "good enough" and that the effort to make changes would require more than they are willing to do. In this scenario, the person is not just *going along* in the same "humdrum" way. Rather, there has been a choice to *not* make a change. Staying the course, or doing nothing different, when it is an *actively processed decision* isn't the same as not doing anything different by default.

All sorts of opportunities are out there. Knowing that piece of information is the first step in coming out of your automatic reactivity and moving into mindfulness. You cannot change something that you are not aware of. Becoming aware is a vital and significant first step that will lead to a transformation from routine to novel, from reactivity to clarity, from dissociation to authenticity. And so, the process of transforming your life from one that merely exists to one that provides a rich sense of contentment and happiness has begun.

6	The Doorway to Freedom: **Choice**	

In the last chapter, I spoke about the importance of realizing that there is an abundance of possibilities and opportunities available to each person. These options exist in every part of your life—in your relationships, at work, within yourself. These alternatives exist at every moment. Without that knowledge, you cannot take the next step of considering different choices. Once you are no longer emotionally engaged and caught up in old patterns, you are free to move outside the realm of what you have always done. You will then be able to think beyond what has always seemed to be your "only choice."

However, just being able to reflect on all possible alternatives will not automatically provide a quick fix and lead to a happy life. You need to know not only what the choices are, but *which ones* will, in fact, lead to consequences that will please you.

As you may have heard it said, "There's generally an up side and a down side to every situation." So, here's the down side: there is no definitive map or magical formula that I can provide for you that will always allow you to make the correct choices. Though I have shared a great deal of my life with you in this book, there is no way for me to share the "perfect potion." The choices I have made along my life's path have been ones that were helpful to *me*. Since each of you is unique, the choices you make must be personally meaningful for *you*. One choice does not fit all. We are born with different personalities and have been raised in diverse environments with different experiences. Even if you were brought up in the same family with very similar circumstances, your perceptions will not be the same.

But here's the up side: each of you has not only the ability, but the power, to connect to yourself and be in touch with what is satisfying, meaningful, and authentic for you. Each of you has the power to create the lives you want. There is no science to it, but there is an art that can be mastered–*The Art of Choice.*

I can help you learn the art and become a master of your choices. The first step is to recognize that your reactions are *yours*. In all my years of working as a therapist, I have never heard or read anything that leads me to believe that there is such a thing as an alien invasion of feelings. The feelings and the reactions you have are yours. Sure, there could very well be a situation that often triggers a certain feeling in you.

Let's revisit again the fact that there are issues from your childhood that you encode in your mental and physical memory. These issues play a major role and act as filtering systems for events that take place in your life. The earlier the incident occurs, the more devastating the impact. (That's because as children you don't have the ability to "think out" a situation. Rather, you respond to it experientially.) In the therapeutic world these are called *core issues.* In popular language, it's your "baggage." So, if something happens that *feels* the same to you as the original incident, there will be an emotional response that comes up rather quickly. Throughout my years as a therapist, I have come to believe that these core issues never totally go away. The emotions that come up are going to come up. However, what you *do* with that emotion is a *choice.*

When I work with clients, it is important that they understand where their feelings are coming from. It is also important that they accept the feelings they have. Many people are not comfortable with the negative or painful feelings and go to great lengths trying not to feel them. Often there are attempts at using different distractions—anything from keeping busy all the time to using alcohol or drugs. The end result is a disconnection from oneself. For some, the cutting off process has taken place early in life and comes out as having a very limited number of emotions. It is certainly healthy to have many different feelings. To exist without experiencing a range of feelings indicates being cut off from oneself. So, when emotions manifest, it is necessary to embrace them. However, you do not have to be a slave to them. In fact, *you can feel the feeling, but choose to act differently.*

A concrete example may be helpful at this point. Let's say that your father walked out on your mother when you were a child. If you are like most children, this was awful and felt as if you had been walked out on, too. Additionally, as a child, you were likely to feel that your father's actions were your fault. This, then, becomes your filtering system for future relationships. As an adult, you get involved with someone and the same filtering system is operating. Your partner says or does something you don't like and it triggers the same sense of abandonment you felt as a child. You feel lousy, or insecure, or angry, or any other number of negative experiences. To have such a reaction is quite understandable. However, it is most likely that the present day situation is not the same as the old one—*it just feels that way.* So, have the feeling, accept it, embrace it, have compassion for the little child who is recalling that old unhappiness. But—you do not have to then take an action based on the feeling as if it had reality in the here and now. To decide not to take that action is the first mindful choice. Once you can recognize that you are having a feeling from the past, and then disengage from it, you have broken out of your mindless reactivity.

You have taken the important step to considering how to handle the situation. You are moving along the path of making a choice. And, you now have the possibility of exploring what choice will serve you best.

In all candor, once a feeling from the past surfaces, it may take a bit of time for it to clear. It could even take a few days. Stay with the feeling—by that I mean, do not try to push it away. If you try to push it away or down or out, you haven't really accepted it; you haven't allowed it to flow. And the consequence will be that the same feeling will still press to be expressed in some form. You might end up yelling at someone for no reason, or you might find yourself eating an entire box of cookies, or you might even end up getting physically ill. Unexpressed feelings do not just go away. However, if you just go with it in an *understanding* way, the emotion will pass. When it does, you will be clearer—this is *disengaging* from it. When you act based strictly on your feelings, the behaviors you manifest are irrational. Not only are they possibly hurtful to another, they do not serve you best. You may actually reflect upon these behaviors, at a later point, and regret them.

I often tell my clients that if something really gets to you, and you can't let go of it, and you go on and on about what was done to you and how the other person made you feel this or that, it is almost for certain that the issue is *yours*.

Once you have let go of an issue that was bothering you, it is time to consider what other possibilities exist for you in response to the upsetting situation. Think about all the different ways you can deal with the situation at hand. If you have some difficulty, reflect on how other people you know might act in a similar set of circumstances. Then write a list of all your alternatives. If you can't come up with any ideas right now, leave it alone and come back to it a little later.

Once you have some possible choices, it will be very helpful to use your imagination. I offer this in the way of an exercise to help you decide which of your possible alternatives will be "right" for you:

Exercise #3: Discovering Possible Alternatives

1. Create some quiet time for yourself by taking yourself away from the busyness of your normal routine. Allow about 10-15 minutes for this exercise. Start by doing some slow, deep breathing. Relax your body. Check in with yourself and scan your body to make sure you are relaxed. If something feels tight, bring your breath to that area to remove the tension.

2. Now, imagine the situation that upset you and one by one plug in the various choices you have considered. As you explore each one, notice your body. Is it getting tense? If so, that choice is not the right one for you.

3. Do some thoughts pop into your head that make you think you ought to make that choice anyway? If so, then reflect back on where those thoughts are coming from and let them go.

4. On the other hand, if your body stays relaxed, that choice is likely to be a good one.

Use this process until you become really comfortable with it. In other words, although a particular choice seemed okay, and your body stayed relaxed, still consider some of the other choices. After eliminating the ones that clearly don't feel right, go back over the "good" ones and retest them.

Now comes the hard part. Take action. For many people, that will amount to taking a risk. It will mean coming out of your comfort zone. What fears come up for you? Are the concerns realistic?

Additionally, there may be times when you will make a choice that ends up not really getting the results you want. When this happens, many people end up feeling that you have made a bad choice. For some, you will feel defeated and even frozen in your actions. I have come to learn that there are no *bad* choices. I consider any choice a good one as long as I can reflect back on it and learn from it. In my experience, the only choices that aren't productive are the ones that have not brought you satisfaction, but you leave unexplored as to why. Experiences that do not lead to beneficial results are wonderful opportunities to learn and further refine your process.

The Art of Choice is a constant ongoing process. As you make a choice and act on it, you must be self-observant. Did it, in fact, lead to a positive outcome? How will you know? Was there a lack of tension? Did the people involved with you also seem to be okay, rather than defensive or uptight? Did further interaction go smoothly? Rather than drama, you will experience a sense of being grounded and connected. You will feel good about yourself.

Of course, all sorts of possibilities will become available as you become more comfortable with this process. At any given moment, your world can expand and offer you seemingly new situations. The truth is that they were always there. What is new is your openness and willingness to consider them.

PART II

THE ART OF CHOICE EXERCISES

<table>
<tr><td>

7

</td><td>

In Relation to Self

</td><td>

</td></tr>
</table>

Introduction

After I had gone through my own journey and learned ways to release myself from my knee-jerk responses to my past, I came across some scientific research that really blew me out of the water. Not only did it validate what I had learned on my own, but it gave scientific meaning to all the reactions I was having. It was the "proof" of the theory so many psychologists refer to, that we all have our "baggage."

It turns out that your issues are actually hard-wired into your brain! (Dan Siegel & Mary Hartzell in *Parenting From the Inside Out*, 2003.) Your brain is the organ that helps you integrate the outer world with your inner world. It is the organ that helps you make sense of what is happening around you. When an incident occurs, the brain responds to it through a neurochemical reaction to help you make meaning of it and also to remember it.

A concrete example may help. As a baby is breast feeding, there are lots of things going on: the baby is being fed, the baby is aware of the mom's scent, the baby is being held. This entire experience is not only occurring but being wired into the brain. If the experience is pleasant, in other words, the mother is smiling at the baby while feeding and holding the baby in a firm and secure way, the experience in wired in as a pleasant one. Conversely, if the mother's attention is consistently drawn elsewhere, if the holding is too tight or not securely enough, the feeding will not be wired in as pleasant. According to Dan Siegel, this becomes an implicit memory. It is a memory that is stored at a cellular level and has meaning for later life.

However, it is not a memory that can be recalled as to when it was explicitly learned.

Here's another example: A little girl is walking down the street with her daddy. She goes to take his hand just at the precise moment that his hand is swinging back. His hand accidentally happens to hit her in the head. Children respond to the world experientially. They are not able as yet to think out the world—to reason it out intellectually. So, what the brain wires in for this little girl is the experiential sense that "when I try to be close to daddy, he pushes me away." Regardless of this inaccuracy of what really took place, the experience gets hard wired into the child's brain. Not only does it get wired in, but it filters future experiences—it will read things in the future according to what it has wired in. So, being very simplistic, many years later, this now adult girl hesitates to be affectionate because she fears being rejected.

Now, here's the tricky part. She doesn't know why she has this fear. She just truly believes she will be rejected. Implicit memory clearly shapes how you respond but you do not remember the specifics of it. It is unlike explicit memory where you can point to exactly when you learned something. Most of you, for example, can remember when you learned the multiplication tables. Implicit memory is a part of you—it is all that surrounded an experience at the time it was happening and you bring it into any present day situation that *feels* the same to you. The brain reads present day situations as the same and triggers the implicit memory. You just don't realize that it's the implicit memory rather than the situation that is presently happening. You truly believe it is the present situation. Since there's no actual memory of something in the past and it feels so real in the here and now, you believe it *is* in the here and now.

As a therapist, there is one way in particular that I know when a client is having a reaction that is an implicit memory. When I point out the reality of the situation, the person can't let it go. Conversely, when the client is merely misunderstanding something about a present day reality and I show that to them, they can let it go. In other words, I can point out an alternate possibility that they can accept as plausible and no longer be upset.

Of course, I have learned to identify this within myself as well. And, so can you!

So, now of course, the question is, what do you do with this? This is where the whole notion of choice comes in. Again, you can't work with anything unless you are aware of it. Once you start to realize that you are reacting with an implicit memory, there are a couple of ways to go. Many times, I offer my clients the analogy of a Microsoft windows program. You are looking at a window, but you can move it over and see that there is another window underneath it. So, think of your immediate reaction as the window you are looking at. Move it over and what is underneath is the reality.

Even though you are having the reaction, the emotional feelings, act in spite of it, based on the reality. In other words, though you are aware that you are experiencing an implicit memory, make the choice to act based on the here-and-now rather than the old feelings. According to Siegel, what you are doing is changing your attention, your focusing, away from the implicit memory. He says that by continuing to focus on the new reality, one is making a *new* neural connection. If one continues to do this process, the old connections wither away and new connections are formed!

I have found that for some people merely refocusing, as Siegel suggests, is not enough. Therefore, I recommend doing the visualizations I have explained previously (Exercise #2: Quieting the Noisy Mind) between the small self you and the adult self you in order to identify your underlying feelings. But again, once you know that it is an implicit memory that is being activated (your buttons are getting pushed), choose to change your focus.

Can this be done? Absolutely! Is it easy? Not at first. Every cell in your body truly believes that your initial, automatic experience is real. It feels so real! And remember, it is cellular memory. But you are being tricked. Know this, believe this, "work" this. Again, what I tell my clients is that if you've never worked out physically and you go to a gym, it's going to be hard at first. You may even think you can't do it. But if you stay at it, little by little, it becomes easier and you see the results. Just like an initially heavy weight becomes easier to lift with time, so will the process of not responding to the sensations of the implicit memory become easier with the more often you do it.

A self-help book is only helpful if there are suggestions in it that offer you specific ways to make changes. The section that follows is devoted to the exercises that will assist you in achieving that goal. After being in practice for over 20 years, I have found that there are some typical bumps or common themes that clients experience in their attempt to living a richer life. What follows are those typical roadblocks and the exercises to get past them. The exercises are a compilation from many sources: things that have worked for me personally in my own growth; ideas I have learned through other resources and have then implemented with clients; and ideas I have come up with as I have worked with individuals. What is consistent throughout is that these are all strategies that have been tried and found to work.

I do suggest that everyone start with the first exercise, *The Main Idea,* to grasp the general concept of what happens to you as a child. After you fully understand that concept, look the others over. Most likely, if you are just starting the process of learning about yourself, you will want to carefully go through the Exercises to help you start to make changes (Tools for Changing). Some of you may already know some of these tools and can be selective or only need to freshen up on your tools. Pick and choose the Exercises as they pertain to you.

Once you have become more tuned into yourself, you will be more sensitive to where *your* particular roadblocks are. In other words, where in your life do you find difficulty? In my experience, people generally tend to have blockages either internally or externally. When there is an internal problem, it manifests in things like fears or having difficulty in some variation of expressing your emotions. When the concern is more of an external one, it results in how you respond to others. I have grouped the exercises according to these categories.

Clearly, you do not live in a vacuum. Your automatic life patterns also include how you interact with others. Conversely, the people in your life have become accustomed to who you *have* been with them and how you *have* functioned in your interactions with them. And so, very often when you make a change, the pattern with others becomes disrupted. I feel that if I only assist you in making changes within yourself, without preparation for possible reactions to that change, I would not be giving you a complete package. Therefore, there are also exercises to help you to deal with issues that may come up for you as you actually go through the change process.

I want to emphasize that there are two methods that I have found to be the most useful in helping people in their healing process—*visualizations* and *free association writing*. Both are utilized throughout the exercises. As a child, you may not have had the opportunity to express your feelings to an unconditional parent. This could have been because your parents were limited themselves, due to their own unresolved issues. Or, somehow you got the message that it wasn't okay to do whatever it was you did. Unexpressed feelings become internalized. They don't go away and they become part of the implicit memory that can be triggered later on. These feelings need to be expressed, they need to be "heard." Both the visualizations and free association writing serve this purpose. As an example, in the earlier "Quieting" visualization, the "small you" is experiencing being loved unconditionally when the "adult you" merely listens to the small you. In uncensored free association writing, your unexpressed, bottled-up feelings are finally being released.

I do want to add one cautionary note: personal growth is a *process*—it does not happen overnight. These Exercises will need to be practiced over time, and more than just once.

I have shared several of my discoveries and breakthroughs with you. It is my hope that I have given you the encouragement to believe that your life offers great promise for the future. You do not have to live out the rest of your years in the same rut or old patterns of your past.

I wish you my best in your endeavors and growth!

The Main Idea

Many people are not loved unconditionally as they grow up. Instead, the love you received from your parents was based (or at least seemed to have been based) on what you *did*, or how you *acted,* rather than just because you existed.

Instead of saying, "I love you just because you are my daughter/son," most parents will say something like, "I love you because... you're such a big help to Mommy," or "...you act so grown up," or "...you always make me laugh," or "... you do so well in school." The list could go on and on indefinitely. Though most parents offer these statements as compliments, the message the child will hear is that these are the *conditions* upon which parental love is based. Thus, these are the *ways* that a child will be able to gain a sense of worthiness.

At an early age, every child learns what to do in order to gain parents' approval. So, for most children, they will learn "to do." What works in childhood is then maintained into adulthood. As an adult, someone who has experienced that the only way to have their parents accept them is by *doing* something will still believe that the only way to feel worthwhile is to prove themselves through "doing." For example, you might find yourself giving up the only free hour you have on the weekend for yourself to take your mother shopping because she mentioned she could use a new coat. Or, you volunteer to pick up Aunt Mary and Uncle Joe for the wedding, even though it takes you an hour out of your way, because you know (or hope) that it will please your parents.

But this is just a habitual pattern that has been learned in your childhood. Therefore, your behavior will always focus on trying to experience a sense of worthiness through *others*. It clearly runs counter to being connected to yourself. It stands in the way of knowing yourself, because there is a need to be aware of others' reactions and to adjust yourself accordingly. In other words, you're so busy worrying about what will make Mom and Dad happy, or at least not upset with you that you haven't got the time, or haven't figured out, whether or not what you're doing is truly what makes *you* happy. Does it truly feel good to run countless errands for your folks? Or are there other things you'd rather be doing, and running errands for them is only a way to not feel guilty, or avoid a conflict, or because that's just what you do?

Exercise #4: The Main Idea

1. Think about all the activities that occupy your daily living.

2. Are they things you truly want to do?

3. What would happen if you didn't do some of them?

4. What are the fears or concerns that you have about not doing them?

5. Where did you learn that doing these things is important?

6. Can and will you stop doing them? Or, can you find a way to do them so that they serve your happiness?

Awareness

In order to break away from old patterns, it is necessary to be aware of them. You cannot change something that you are not aware of. But sometimes, being aware doesn't necessarily clear them. Remember that the reactions and behaviors are very ingrained. You have been doing them for several years and they have become habitual. So, it may take more than knowledge of the patterns to shake them loose.

One technique that may help you to understand what is driving a particular reaction in you, and your consequential behavior, is to think about how you would feel if you didn't do it. Imaging the situation with a different ending can be very freeing.

Exercise #5: Awareness

1. Imagine a particular upsetting situation—what feelings come up for you?

2. Is there someone else's reaction to your not acting a certain way that creates discomfort?

3. Are you concerned about how people will view you if you don't function as you have in the past?

4. Do you anticipate a loss of some type?

5. Are there any fears attached to not doing what you always have (other than coming out of your comfort zone)?

6. What do you imagine would happen if you didn't do what you usually do in response to the situation?

Noticing Your Body

The more you become aware of your body, the more you will be able to notice your different reactions. These reactions can serve as signals to you as to what you are really feeling. Only as you become aware of something can you make the choice to change it.

As examples, in my therapy sessions, I started to realize that my bodily reactions were indications of what was going on with the client. If I suddenly felt tired, it meant that the client had unexpressed anger—the tiredness I experienced was the energy that was being used to keep my feelings from being expressed. Another client may tend to over think or obsess about an issue. Though it appears he is just trying to think it through, it's really a defensive intellectualization to avoid what he is really feeling. When someone is doing that, I start to get a headache.

Regardless of the fact that each person's body may have its own "language" as expressed in different reactions, everyone's body does speak to them in some way. Initially, you may still act in ways that are reflective of old patterns—the trick is to stop the automatic nature of it and make a change. Your body can be a wonderful source of information as to when you are reacting to something. If no reaction is going on, if you are flowing, your body will be relaxed. So, if you feel your body tighten up, it's letting you know that there's something you need to pay attention to. This will then free you up to make a new choice rather than get caught up in the same old business.

Exercise #6: Noticing Your Body

1. Think back on a situation that has upset you. Play it over in your mind. When you really have a sense that you are "back there," scan your body and notice how it feels.

2. Are there other times you have the same sensations?

3. Are there times you have different sensations? In other words, do certain types of situations seem to evoke feelings in your stomach whereas other scenarios bring on a headache?

4. Is there some pattern to what your body feels and what is going on?

5. If you are not sure of what you are feeling, you can try the "Quieting" visualization I suggested in Chapter Four between the small child part of you and the adult part of you. You can also have your body "write a letter" to you and let you know why it's feeling a certain way. To do this, start by writing, "Dear (your name)," and make a statement regarding the symptoms you have been experiencing. Then, continue to write, in a free association way, why those symptoms are there. What purpose are they serving? What lessons are you supposed to be learning? What is your body trying to tell you that you have not been paying attention to?

6. When you are done, read what you wrote. What feelings have been expressed that you haven't been paying attention to? You might want to do the "Quieting" visualization to respond to them. Or perhaps, your body is telling you that you've been "on the go" too much and need to relax.

Observing Your Behavior

Another way to become aware of moments when you are merely reacting to an old pattern is to become observant of your behavior in different situations. If you start to notice that people in various situations are reacting to you similarly, it is likely *you* are doing something to create that.

Jim, one of my clients, often found himself getting into squabbles with his coworkers. At first, he would complain about something they did or didn't do. Jim then ended up feeling, in some way, that he was not understood, or that he was treated unfairly. This happened at his full-time teaching job as well as at his summer job. After Jim retired, he took a part-time job. The same thing began happening there. I suggested he look at what *he* was doing that might be creating the similar reactions he was getting in three distinct environments.

Once Jim was willing to acknowledge that the same thing was happening in the three different situations, where the people were totally unrelated, he was willing to look at his behavior. Furthermore, he went on to explore what was consistent for him as far as the underlying feelings. In doing so, he recognized that in each of the three situations, he had the sense that he was not being recognized, or seen as worthy. This feeling was very familiar to him from his childhood. Having identified this dynamic, he was now able to embrace his feelings, but not act upon them as if they had any reality in the present.

If you find a similar scenario happening to you time after time, it's unlikely that everyone else is to blame.

Exercise #7: Observing Your Behavior

1. Start to observe if you are left with similar feelings or reactions, even though the particulars of situations are varied as are the people in those situations.

2. Ask yourself whether there is a common underlying feeling associated with these diverse situations—feelings that somehow remind you of things or people from your past?

3. In the past, how did you respond?

4. Are you doing something similar now?

5. Are the situations today truly the same as what happened in the past?

6. Are there other possibilities as to why others that you are interacting with might be doing the things they are (other than your preconceived notions)?

7. Remember that you are no longer a powerless child—you have the choice to do something different. In what other ways can you respond to the irritating situations, in order to generate a different outcome?

Noting Your Thoughts

You are accustomed to seeing the world through your filtering system. Therefore, it is likely that you'll react to situations that you perceive as similar in a consistent way. Your filtering mechanism has been in place since your childhood. So, not only are your reactions based on it, you also anticipate upcoming events through that same mechanism.

To break free from your old patterns, it is helpful to become aware of your thoughts that occur *before* an actual uncomfortable situation takes place. You may not even realize that you are having the thoughts that set the stage for what is to come. These negative expectations set up a self-fulfilling prophecy. That is, if you expect something to happen, you are primed for it, and you're more likely to see what you expect. You will then react consistently. The other person will respond based on the way you've reacted. You then will respond to the response and the end result is exactly what you expected to occur.

Here's a concrete example: As a college teacher, if I'm aware that a student has come to class late several times, there are a number of possible thoughts that might possibly occur to me. If, in my past, I have felt disrespected (let's say by my parents), my likely assessment is that this student is being disrespectful to me. I might make a snide remark to the student. Having been offended by my remark, the student responds defensively, perhaps sarcastically. Aha! I presume that I am right. The student clearly is disrespectful.

But here's another possible scenario: What if the student is from a poor family with only one car that must be shared? Before coming to school, she first has to drop her father off at work. What if this is this the reason she is always late? In this case, the student is not acting out of disrespect as I'd thought. Rather, she is simply taking her father to work so she has a car to get to school. In this instance, she clearly is not being disrespectful.

This example is easy to comprehend. However, a very similar process of making snap judgments happens daily on a more profound and pervasive scale. Without knowing it, each person is constantly making assumptions about the reasons for other people's behavior. You seldom check it out, and you usually act according to what it is you have assumed. The other person reacts to you, also without checking out why you have acted as you have. Once again, you respond back. And so on, and so on, and so on. Assumption upon assumption, error, upon error, each of you continues. And do not forget that a great majority of your assumptions are not based on reality, but rather on your past.

In order to have a life that flows smoothly, it is important to avoid negatively anticipating the future. Instead, start to approach uncomfortable situations in a detached way—more like an observer, holding your emotions at bay. It is by letting go of the emotional arousal, which stands in the way of clear thinking, that you can stay open to other possibilities.

Exercise #8: Noting Your Thoughts

1. Very often, thoughts are the by-products of emotions. Think back to a situation that was unpleasant. What emotions did the situation stir in you?

2. Start to become aware of the thoughts that play over and over again in your head that are at a sub-level of awareness (almost like "white" noise). These are often self-critical or self-blaming thoughts.

3. Were these thoughts present as you entered the situation?

4. What were you expecting to happen?

5. Are there experiences from your past that have created the foundation for these thoughts?

6. Do they make sense in the here and now?

7. When these thoughts come up, literally change the thought—make yourself think of anything else. Initially, this will be difficult and the thought will come back. With practice, however, it will become easier to do and the old thought will no longer be a menace.

8 Responding to Particular Blockages

Releasing Fear

Many people still have a particular fear even though they know that it is irrational. Some people can state when the fear started, others are clueless. Certain fears are very contained, that is, they only occur in a specific situation. For example, someone might have a fear of a black cat. They will be fine around all other animals, they will even be fine around other cats, just as long as it is not black. Conversely, there are some fears that are pervasive—they extend into many different situations. Such a fear would be agoraphobia, which is a fear of going into public places where there is no easy means of escape. Clearly, the latter is far more devastating. Regardless of how the fear manifests, it is a blockage of energy and will often stand in the way of one's full functioning.

Exercise #9: Dealing with Fear

1. If you are in a situation that is fearful for you, acknowledge what is happening.

2. Remind yourself that it is an old issue that does not have meaning in the present.

3. Begin breathing slowly, and make the choice to no longer give this fear power over you. Declare that it is no longer meaningful. Concentrate on your breath—bring it in deeply to your solar plexus. Physiologically, by breathing and relaxing, you are creating a condition that is counter to fear. With continued practice, as a combination of creating a relaxation response in your body and a corrected cognition, over time, the intensity of this fear will dissipate.

By doing this breathing and releasing the energy of the fear, you are connecting to your grounded self. By breathing and consciously choosing to let go of this fear, there will be less focus on the thought and greater focus on your sense of feeling empowered.

Here's another approach to dealing with a fear that you know is irrational:

Exercise #10: Alternate Approach to Fear

1. Accept that the fear is there.

2. However, act regardless of the fear. Just do it.

3. When you see that you have been able to do whatever it is you feared, it helps to alleviate it. The action you have taken serves to remind you that you can, in fact, do that which you feared. Therefore, it creates a new foundation for you to act upon in the future.

In the future, when the same fear arises, remind yourself that when you took action the last time, things turned out okay. You'll notice that this time, the action will be a little easier to do; there won't be as much fear involved. Little by little, this process will help you build a new sense of confidence that will eventually lead you to a point of self-trust.

Not Detaching From Yourself

You will be aware of the common addictions—drinking, drugging, gambling, "sexing." In recent years, these have come to be known as the hard addictions. There are other behaviors that are also addictive—workaholism, perfectionism, procrastination, eating disorders.

In some way, each of these addictions allow you to disconnect from your feelings. When you engage in these behaviors, you are escaping from truly dealing with what you feel.

I've also observed that when people obsess about something, worry about an issue over and over again, it is a way to distract themselves from something they do not want to look at. Sometimes this obsessing will take the form of constantly finding fault with someone else. This certainly avoids taking responsibility for your behavior. It also serves as a barrier to emotional intimacy with that person.

Exercise #11: Staying Focused

1. Is your life out of balance? Is there too much emphasis in one area to the exclusion of others?

2. Do you find yourself overly concerned about something and not able to let go of it?

3. What might you be avoiding?

4. If you didn't do this activity, what thoughts or feelings would come up?

5. When I notice that a client is addictive or obsessing, I suggest they sit without any distractions for 15-20 minutes. No phones, no radio, no TV, no reading—just sit. For such people, it doesn't take long for the uneasy feelings to emerge. When they emerge for you, sit for another few minutes to intensify the discomfort. Now, do free association writing. Just write—don't think about what you're writing. Spelling and grammar don't count. This exercise will help reveal what you are hiding from.

6. Once you know the feelings that you have not addressed, start to do your small self/your adult self "Quieting" visualization on a regular basis. Generally, obsessing is a way of avoiding unpleasant feelings. They may be emotions like sadness, pain, or guilt. When these previously unattended feelings are responded to in the visualization, the need to obsess will lessen.

Letting Yourself Express Emotions

In life there are always going to be bumps and difficult situations. And, it is quite normal to have reactions to them. Learning The Art of Choice does not mean you won't have reactions. It means you will learn how to recognize your automatic reactions and be able to make clear choices as to what positive actions you want to take.

Many clients I've worked with will tell me how much something has upset them. They'll go on and on telling me how bothered they are. Though the words are there, no feelings are being exhibited. When people do this, they are intellectualizing. That is, they are talking from their heads and only their heads. It's as if they have disconnected from themselves, from their emotions.

Here's another type of possible manifestation: one client always complained that her spouse was without emotion. After I had worked with him, it turned out that just the opposite was true. He had a great deal of emotionality but was very uncomfortable expressing it. Of course, he was not aware of this. Though he looked like he was dumb to a lot of situations, in fact, he was numb! Think about it this way: if you rest your arm on a chair, initially you might experience pins and needles. If you don't remove your arm, the increase in sensation makes your arm feel numb.

Just because emotions do not get expressed does not mean that they don't exist or are lying dormant.

In fact, unexpressed emotions, even unacknowledged ones, can cause a person to react to unpleasant situations. Like a volcano that may be inactive at the moment, they can one day suddenly become active and erupt intensely as in an argument. Or, the reaction may be more passively expressed, as sarcasm. And even if someone doesn't outwardly react, the emotions can create blocks that prevent them from responding clearly to a situation at hand. Since emotions always override cognition, when someone is blocked, they will not be able to think things out clearly. So, though they may seem fine on the outside, they may be experiencing a sense of fuzziness internally. And even if they are not experiencing the fuzziness, it may be manifested in their behavior in such things as not being able to follow a conversation or having difficulty doing simple math on a restaurant check.

I have also found that people who have learned to turn off their emotions find it very frightening when they start to experience them. Many people will tell me that they think that they are going to go out-of-control or are afraid that they will not be able to function. Let me assure you that the expression of emotion will not place you into a state of dysfunction. I usually recommend taking yourself out of your comfort zone slowly and seeing that it's okay.

Exercise #12: Expressing Emotions

1. When something upsets you, are you aware that you are also feeling it in your body?

2. Do you merely relate the incident without letting yourself also acknowledge your feelings about it?

3. Have you been taught as you grew up to not let your feelings out? (Little boys are especially prone to this.)

4. Have you been made to feel that you're being too sensitive if you outwardly express your emotions?

5. Being in touch with your emotions is not the same thing as creating lots of drama. But it is essential to be able to identify your feelings if you are attempting to change them.

6. Your emotions need to be expressed. Use either the "Quieting" visualization or free association writing to allow this to happen.

7. Do this process slowly. Do it over and over again.

Accepting Your Feelings

You may have found that unpleasant feelings have been so painful that you have totally cut them off from your awareness. Since fear is such a strong emotion and one you need for survival, usually you remain in touch with that emotion. But there may be a host of other feelings that you are denying, or simply avoiding. Perhaps there is a sense of sadness or the pain of feeling abandoned or lost. In the past, you have probably found some technique to avoid experiencing the discomfort of these feelings. You have probably gotten so good at managing these unpleasant feelings that you do so automatically, and have become unaware that they are there. As you start to become more aware of yourself, it is also likely that these old feelings will resurface.

Initially, you may be uncomfortable or even concerned when you start to feel those old emotions coming up. It could make you will feel like you are in a fog. Emotions do "overtake" you, they do seem to override your thinking. I used to say I felt like I had clouds in my head.

Do not be alarmed or worry that you are going out-of-control. Keep in mind that these are just memories of the past that have been internalized. The only thing that is different is that you are now consciously aware of them.

Certainly, it is difficult to re-experience painful memories. In order to avoid feeling them, people tend to try to push them away or to distract themselves. The problem with doing this is that the memory does not actually go away, it only gets suppressed temporarily.

Rather than attempting to make the memory go away, I suggest that you welcome it. There is a reason the experience has lingered. When it happened to you as a child, no one responded in a caring or loving way. Thus, if you continue to ignore the feeling, you are merely perpetuating the original hurt.

Exercise #13: Accepting Your Feelings

1. Do the "Quieting" visualization between the "small self" you and the "adult self" you. Picture yourself as a young child expressing yourself to yourself as you are now.

2. Let the feelings be expressed in whatever way is comfortable: with words, with body language, with gestures, with facial expressions, even telepathically.

3. Just let them be expressed, sit with them, embrace them. They cannot hurt you any more; they are just memories from your past.

4. You are no longer a helpless child. The more you attempt to get rid of them, the more intense they are likely to become. These are feelings that you have locked away. They have been waiting "to be heard." The more you can flow with them, the faster they will quiet down.

5. Let the adult self you just take in the information—don't try to fix it or explain it.

6. When the small self is done, let the adult self go to eye level and say to the small self, "I love you."

Since your core issues are very entrenched, you will probably need to do this process several times. But the more you practice it, the easier both the process and your life will become. Over time, the feelings will not manifest as raw or wounded, and you will get triggered less often and less intensely.

Controlling Impulsivity

Many people will admit that they have a quick temper or a short fuse. Clients have reported to me that their emotional reactions can "go from zero to 60" instantaneously. But through my work over the years, what I've found is that these people think they are going out of control so quickly because they are really unaware of themselves. In fact, if they were more mindful (aware) of their own reactions, they would be picking up the signals that would let them know they are starting to get upset. In being out of touch with themselves, they are missing the important cues that will tip them off. It is similar to a driver who gets so distracted while speaking on his or her cell phone that the sign for the exit needed is missed; a foolish attempt to get off the highway is made, often times creating or almost creating an accident.

If you are the kind of person who realizes that you are volatile, that you react too quickly, then you need to pay more attention to your body and to your thoughts. Of course, if you are not accustomed to picking up your bodily signals, you will not be able to do so at the moment that something unpleasant is happening. You will need to learn to do this.

I tell clients that if you volunteer to help a friend move, you are not going to be able to lift the very heavy boxes just because you've said you're willing to help. In order for you to have the necessary physical strength, you would need to have already started to build up your muscles.

Exercise #14: Controlling Impulsivity

1. To help you start to notice your body, take a moment to notice how your body is feeling two or three times during the day.

2. Is there tightness? Is there tension?

3. It doesn't matter where you are or what you are doing—just take stock of how your body feels.

4. After doing this for a while, when these sensations are present, you will begin to consciously notice them. If you are in a situation in which your body starts to feel tense, do not ignore it. Stop and pay attention to the sensations. This will give you the opportunity to take action, at this early point, and before it builds up to where you lose control.

5. One of the best ways to deal with the uncomfortable feeling once you notice it is to use the free association writing technique. Not only will there be a release of feelings, but what you write will help you see what's really upsetting you.

6. 6. If you are in the middle of an interaction with someone and you notice that you are starting to react, just excuse yourself. If it's someone you're not close to, pretend you have to use the facilities. If it is someone with whom you're close, let them know you need to take a moment for yourself.

9 In Relation to Others

Being Okay Without a Partner

Many people believe that you cannot feel happy in life unless you are part of a couple. In large part, this is because of the way our society is set up—we are a couples' society. You are often given the message that in order to be worthy, in order to feel satisfied or "complete," you must be involved with someone. You see it in our commercials, in our movies, in our books, and hear it in our songs.

Though being part of a partnership has its rewards, a relationship alone is not the solution to your happiness and sense of self-worth. It is not the magic bullet. A relationship can enhance your life—enhance not create. But, in order to really feel good with someone, you must first feel good within yourself. In order to be intimate with someone—to be open and non-judgmental—you must first be intimate with yourself. It is very difficult to be truly loving to someone else when you do not feel that way about yourself. By being in connection to yourself and learning to accept yourself, you will be better able to offer the same to someone else. How do you give what you don't have?

Exercise #15: Creating Intimacy with Yourself

1. Understand that you have many different parts, or aspects, to yourself.

2. Make a list and identify as many different aspects of yourself as you can. For example, the funny part, the intelligent part, the shy part, the athletic part, the stubborn part, etc.

3. Reflect on the concept that in order for an orchestra to achieve its beautiful, rich sound, it needs the input of all the varied sounds of the different instruments. Individually, like the cello, they might not sound as enjoyable.

4. Close your eyes and visualize all your different parts. As the adult you, go to each part of you and take a few moments to acknowledge it, smile at it, embrace it, make sure that each part knows that they are loved and valued.

5. Go back to your list and acknowledge that each part has both an "upside" and "downside" to it. For example, the stubborn side can be useful in situations that require standing up for yourself when someone is trying to get you to do something you'd rather not do.

6. As you practice this, you will start to feel comfortable, and more loving to who you are, as you are.

Automatic Reactions to Others

If you find that there is someone close to you who is upsetting you over and over again, it is very likely that the behavior of the person is really reminding you of something from your past. In other words, someone without your past would not necessarily be bothered by the same behavior.

Many of my clients involved in relationships have complained about behaviors that their mates do, or don't do, that they find particularly bothersome. Though they will point to specific behaviors, with a little exploration they find the underlying feelings of their own that these behaviors are tapping into. Themes start to emerge. Furthermore, the behaviors that tend to be habitually upsetting are those that are triggering feelings from the past.

Exercise #16: Reactions to Others

1. Write down a list of your partner's behaviors that bother you.

2. In your mind's eye, actually re-create a situation when your mate did one of these annoying behaviors.

3. Become aware of the feelings that are hooked into these situations.

4. Now, think back to earlier times where you had the same feelings. It is likely that it is these negative episodes in your childhood that got triggered by your mate's behavior.

5. You can do a small self/adult self "Quieting" visualization to deal with the early childhood memories that have come up, or use free association writing to express your feelings of that time. Either one will help you express feelings that have been bottled up until this point. With the "Quieting" visualization, you can also create an imagery of unconditional acceptance of whatever has been expressed.

Breaking Old Patterns

It's often easier to get along with someone you are not close to since you do not have a strong emotional investment in them, or in your interactions with them. That makes it easier to let things go because a strong significance to the relationship doesn't exist. But when you are involved with someone who is close to you, you are more likely to feel vulnerable, and you take things far more personally. You are less objective, you have more at stake, and you are more likely to feel hurt. It's likely that this same process is happening to the other person in your interaction. You then find yourself in the same "dance" with one another—each of you reacting the way you always have and neither of you feeling satisfied.

As you become more accustomed to noticing what's going on in your body, it will become easier to alter the "dance" you've been involved in with your partner, or other loved ones. Remember, if you feel a reaction in your body, it is because you are getting grabbed by some triggered memory. You are responding to old patterns rather than being present, in the moment, about the situation at hand. When you recognize that this is happening to you, you then have the possibility of letting go of the automatic reaction.

You will also be able to notice what is happening for the other person. If they are reacting badly or acting out in some way, it is also likely that they have been triggered, and are reacting to something in their past. By noticing your reaction and the other person's as well, you have the opportunity to "clear" yourself. By "clearing yourself" I mean to bring yourself back into the present moment. Do so by taking a long, slow breath and reminding yourself that whatever reaction you are experiencing is a memory from the past and not about what is happening at this moment. Once you do that, even though you may still be experiencing the sensations, you can respond to the situation at hand, from your adult self. By not responding emotionally, you will not be perpetuating the reactivity of the situation. In fact, you will likely be able to respond to the other person in a more loving way, again remembering that they, too, are reacting out of their past memories. And most likely, the entire interaction will be calmed.

Exercise #17: Clearing Yourself

1. Acknowledge that what you are feeling is from the past.

2. Use deep breathing to release the feelings. Slowly take a breath in from your nose and bring it past your throat, past your chest, and into your solar plexus. Hold it there for a few moments. Then, release the breath through your lips, open just slightly. Do this again very slowly, as if you are blowing at a lit candle where you want the light to flicker but you do not want to blow it out.

3. Even if the feelings don't go completely away, you can still make the choice to take actions that are more appropriate to the actual here-and-now situation even though you are experiencing the sensations from the past.

Once you have cleared yourself, you can offer more validating and loving responses to your loved ones. When you are no longer habitually reacting from your past and can therefore offer a more loving response to others, the cyclical pattern is broken and both of you will find yourselves more open to the possibility of relating in a whole new way.

The more you have cleared yourself, the more available you will be to others, especially the most meaningful people in your life.

To Confront or Not to Confront

Many people feel that when they are upset with someone, they need to confront that person. However, for most them, this results in talking with anger and/or in an attacking manner.

Sometimes, addressing someone about something that is upsetting you can be helpful. But in order for you to get the most out of it, it is important that you first explore where your feelings are coming from, and what your goals are for talking with this person.

Exercise #18: Confronting

1. Ask yourself, is this really the person with whom you are upset, or was the thing that bothered you triggered by something from your past?

2. Clear yourself first and see if the incident still bothers you. (See Exercise #17)

3. If you are still bothered by the incident, and it is truly important for you to straighten it out, consider the possibilities. Why might have the other person acted as they did? In doing this, you will be better able to remain calm and not attack the person. You'll be better able to stay clear as to the different options that will then allow you to have a healthier communication.

4. You must also think about your reason for talking to this person. Is it to try to get them to change? Is it likely that this person will be able to "hear" you?

5. It may be helpful to imagine different scenarios that could play out following the confrontation. Then ask yourself, "Am I prepared to deal with any or all of these different scenarios?" Imagine all the possible responses including the ones you would not like. If you are not prepared to deal with them, you would be better off choosing another plan of action for yourself. Perhaps, you would just want to vent to a close friend about the situation or release the pent up feelings through exercises.

When working with clients who have been abused as children, many therapists feel that in order for the person to heal, they must confront their perpetrator. In all my years of practice, I have not found this to be necessarily true. There is a good chance that the perpetrator will not take responsibility for what has been done. Therefore, the victim is not going to be better off, and is likely to feel re-victimized. Time and again, I have found that healing is quite possible without direct confrontation.

Most people have been free of traumatic abuse and do not have to confront very painful memories. Yet, many people find merely confronting another person about a touchy situation is difficult. Some people even find raising a point of difference difficult to do, like telling someone that they were not happy with the way something happened. Or, it could even be as simple as asking someone to do a favor. These are people who tend to be easy going, don't like "to make waves," are not assertive, and are likely to have a hard time standing up for themselves or those close to them like a spouse or child. Perhaps, the message they got when they were children was that they were not worthy. Or, it is possible that when they did try to speak up, they were met with a great deal of perceived negativity. So, while the degree of trauma is not as extensive, the experience of difficulty is still painful. The process to deal with this type of confrontation is the same as noted above.

10	Moving Forward With Others	

Accepting Our Differences

We all know that all of us are different from one another. And at an intellectual level, we can accept that as a fact. Yet, one of the greatest problems we face in our world is that emotionally we can't allow for those differences. In some instances, when someone is different, you can't seem to help being uncomfortable. From that discomfort arises fear and insecurity. Unfortunately, in order to feel better about yourself, you may create a sense of being better than the other person. Many times, you accomplish this superior feeling by putting the other person down in some way.

I remember one client who told me he felt confident in himself. He also shared with me his awareness that he was condescending to others. I had to educate him to the fact that if he was condescending and had the need to put someone else down, it was a false sense of confidence.

If you find that you are viewing others as less worthy than yourself in some way, chances are you don't really feel good within yourself. Should that be the case, it is another indication of emotional blockage and a habitual reactive pattern. When you feel really safe within yourself, you can easily allow for someone else's differences. You may notice them, but you do not get caught up in, or react to, them.

Exercise #19: Accepting Differences

1. Take a mental survey of the people who are your friends. Are they all similar to you?

2. Being totally candid with yourself, are there some people you do not like?

3. Do these people make you feel uncomfortable?

4. Do you feel or think better or less of yourself in their presence?

5. Do you have negative thoughts or feelings about these people?

6. What are the origins of the impressions you have about these people?

7. If you find that as you answer these questions, you become aware that your self-esteem is in need of some support, do the small self/adult self "Quieting" visualization and make sure the small self feels your adult self love.

Letting Go of Expectations

It is important to learn to let go of your expectations of others, because your expectations are very personally based from your own frame of reference. People are different; each of us is born with different temperaments, each of us is raised in different families; each of us has been exposed to different experiences. I assure you that someone who is important in your life does not wake up in the morning and think about ways to make your life difficult or ways to hurt you. Yet, they may very well do or say things that will be hurtful.

To help you get a grasp of this, it is important to look at the whole picture.

Exercise #20: Letting Go of Expectations

1. Is this person important to you? Remember, different people may be important to you for different reasons. For example, someone may be a great friend to go shopping with, and someone else is terrific as a support system in time of need.

2. Is your relationship with this person a healthy one; that is, do you each feel you gain from it?

3. If you are involved with someone and you are not gaining positive things, you may want to reconsider whether or not you want to keep investing in the relationship. (Keep in mind that you don't necessarily have to give to each other in the same exact way, but each of you must feel that the reward of being in the relationship outweighs the cost.)

4. Look at the bigger picture and start to "let go" of the smaller things that are mere manifestations of differences or imperfections.

5. This is a hard concept for some people. To learn to do this, it's helpful to start thinking things like: "If I were to die tomorrow, would this situation that is bothering me still have any meaning?" or "In 100 years, is whatever upsetting to me still going to be upsetting?" or "If this person were to move to another state far away and I couldn't see them, would I be fine without them?" As you practice thinking this way, it will help to put things in perspective.

6. Learning to meditate can also be helpful in the process of "letting go." One type of meditation, referred to as mindfulness meditation, is a process

where you learn to focus on your breathing and nothing else. Initially, this is difficult to do, but as with everything else, becomes easy with practice. When other thoughts come, as they will, you merely observe them, acknowledge that they are there, but allow them to pass. In other words, you make sure that you do not start to think about these other thoughts or focus on them. If you focus on the other thoughts, you are turning your attention away from your breathing. Once you have learned to meditate, focus on your breath, not pay attention to a thought you have learned to let go. Then, in your everyday life, when something is disturbing, you can use this same process by taking a breath and focusing on it rather than the disturbing thought.

It is also essential to remember that you cannot change another person. However, the good news is that you can change yourself. Once you start doing something different, there is a much greater chance of the interaction between you and another changing as well.

11 Signs of Change

When you go to the gym, you are able to actually see the results of your efforts—you can take measurements, you can look in the mirror, or you can notice that your clothes fit differently. Though the outward markers of change that result from doing the Exercises in this book are far more subtle, the results are far reaching and dramatic. As you may have heard in a commercial many times—the impact on your life "is priceless!"

Change is a process and it happens gradually. As a matter of fact, you might wonder, "How will I know if change is taking place?" Even though the changes are subtle, there are ways of monitoring them. Knowing what to look for will assist you in the process of being self-observant. Also, any time someone encounters change it feels uncomfortable because it is new; it takes a bit of adjustment. The more you know what to expect, the more prepared you will be to deal with "the new you!"

To follow are some indicators to help you know that, in fact, you have been effective in starting your journey.

Rocking the Boat

Oddly enough, one of the ways that will help you know that you have, in fact, made changes is that things that used to seem "okay," to not bother you will start to be upsetting. Remember, you have been functioning on "autopilot." Situations and reactions followed a certain pattern. As you come out of the fog and gain clarity, these very same experiences will start to look differently to you.

Keep in mind that change is often uncomfortable. Anything that is different is usually going to feel strange at first. Once you gain the ability to maintain your clarity and respond to the here-and-now, rather than emotionally to your past, you have the option of exploring the different possibilities available to you. Even if you end up doing the same thing you have always done, now it will be a choice rather than by default.

When there is change, the new ways of being will tend to feel awkward. You will probably not feel sure-footed. You may or may not get support or recognition from others in your life. In fact, you may get some uncomfortable negative reactions from them. Odds are they will not be accustomed to you no longer acting in the usual pattern. It is important that you recognize how your shift may impact others and possibly make them uncomfortable. For example, if you have never asserted yourself and now start to stand up for your rights, it is likely that others will initially respond in a hostile way but with time treat you respectfully. Or, if you have always been a people-pleaser who has over-extended yourself and you start to be more aware of taking care of your needs, the initial response from others might be disappointment until they become accustomed to you deserving to have your needs met also.

Others are reacting to you because they are not accustomed to the shifts you have made. Though you cannot control their reactions, it is possible that they, too, may now shift in response to you and how you now behave. Whether they do or don't, once you realize that there is a shift in the interaction and some possible residual discomfort, it is important that you continue to truly believe in yourself. Know that you have worked hard at shedding old reactive patterns in order to connect to your authentic or core self. Believe in yourself.

Exercise #21: Rocking the Boat

1. It is very important that you acknowledge yourself and be aware of even the small improvements you have made.

2. Reinforce yourself. See each of your accomplishments in a positive light. Praise yourself for whatever strides you have made focusing on the improvements, rather than if there is still more to be done.

3. Look back at how you used to act and what the actual differences are. This will help you to see the progress and know that with time, your small advances will lead to larger ones.

4. Stay in the process of choosing to make changes whenever you see the need. And, also with time, your comfort zone will expand to include your new choices.

The Feeling of Flow

One of the questions that keeps coming up in therapy is, "How am I able to identify when something is no longer an issue for me?" Healing starts to take place after you have done your work—allowed yourself to feel the feelings, allowed yourself to express those feelings and have accepted them. Some issues are so deep and had so much meaning to you when they happened that we call them "core issues." It is unlikely that these feelings will ever totally go away. They will come up—but not as often; and when they do, they will not feel as intense and they will go away more easily.

Many clients have told me that they find it hard to believe that their old issues don't bother them they way they used to. So, what they do is they revisit them. They replay the issue in their minds and notice how they feel. You can do the same. Here are Exercises to guide you through this process:

Exercise #22: Feeling Flow

1. Replay, or think about, an incident that has troubled you in the past.

2. Notice the following: Does your body feel calm with virtually no reaction? Are the old "tapes" that ran through your head now silent? Does it feel like the emotion that had been associated with this incident is absent? If the answer to these questions is "yes," healing has taken place.

3. What you will find is that is possible for you to talk about the incident, since it is a part of your history, but you can do so in an objective way.

You can never take away the past. The past is still something that has happened to you. And you cannot change your past. But what you have changed, what you have taken control over is how much of a slave you have been to your past. By doing these Exercises with full commitment, you have cleared yourself, you have released yourself. There is no more "story." There is no more emotional energy or upset as you either think about it, or tell about it.

You are left with a fully realized YOU and always being AT CHOICE!

Final Note

Remember that core issues don't ever completely go away. These are experiences that happened early in life that you stored in your mental and physical (cellular) memory. These experiences have acted as your filtering systems in the way you perceive situations. In a way, your past assessments serve to protect you in future endeavors. They attempt to look out for you to make sure you don't get hurt again.

Through these pages, you have learned that much of what you felt in the past is, in reality, not totally accurate. But because your reactions happen so fast, you don't always have time to think about them. Even with all the work you have done and will continue to do, there may be times when an old automatic reaction flares up. Many times it will be because of an unanticipated situation. Also, at transitional times in one's life, old issues have to be dealt with again. For example, let's take a woman who has felt insecure in her abilities while growing up. She is likely to re-experience these fears when she gets married, and again when she has a child, and again when she purchases a home.

As a child, there were lots of things that happened to me that left me feeling emotionally abandoned. Through my personal work, I was able to let go of this fear and alter the usual negative manifestations in my behavior. Recently, an uncle who was very dear to me died suddenly and unexpectedly. Aside from the normal, expected grief, I realized that my old abandonment issue had kicked in again.

If you find yourself in a similar situation, do not worry that all your work has been for naught. As I did in the case of my uncle, welcome these old feelings, rather than try to push them away, or be rid of them. To do so will only increase their intensity. The more you flow with your emotions and connect to their meaning, the quicker you will transition through them, and the more control you will feel.

Taking on the work of looking at oneself and making changes requires courage. But the rewards for doing so offer a life that is quite rich. I always tell my clients that even if the old issues come back, they do not come back as often. When they do, they are not as intense, and you'll find you can handle them much more quickly.

Having read this book and practiced the Exercises, you are armed with the process that will allow you to always be able to choose to live your life at choice. I thank you for allowing me to help you in your journey.

You have accomplished something truly wonderful—you have reconnected with the real you and transformed yourself. In so doing, your world is open to endless possibilities for you to explore and enjoy. There's only one more thing left for you to do: claim that which is rightfully mandated to each of you—the joy of living!

About the Author

Karen Sherman, Ph.D., has been in private practice for over 20 years. Her first book, *Marriage Magic! Find It, Keep It, and Make It Last* was originally published in 2004 with co-author Dale Klein. She is a contributing author to *101 Ways to Self-Improvement*, Vol. 2.

Karen is a featured writer on Yahoo Personals, has a weekly blog on ThirdAge.com, and writes the Disputes column for Hitchedmag.com.

She is interviewed regularly in the media including *Men's Health, Family Circle, Self, Women's World, Long Island's Newsday, Crain's NY* and others. She is a frequent guest on talk radio stations, both nationally and internationally.

Dr. Sherman conducts a variety of workshops on relationships and lifestyle issues at Westchester Community College; Queensborough Community College, Roslyn Continuing Education; YEO - Albany Chapter; Knowledge Network-Albany, NY; and Pathways - Manhasset, NY. She also hosts her own teleseminars as well as through a leading NYC PR company.

She's a frequent speaker at Clubhouse of Suffolk, ILR at Farmingdale State University, Returning students program at CW Post, and various NY area libraries, and is a member of a national speakers' service.

Additionally, Dr. Sherman serves on the faculty at CW Post University. Her memberships include American Psychological Association, American Counseling Association, Nationally Board Certified Counselor and she is a Certified National Family Life Educator and belongs to the National Registry for Marriage Friendly Therapists.

Karen resides on Long Island, NY, is married and has two daughters. In her spare time, Karen enjoys reading, traveling, and playing Suduko.

About our Series Editor, Robert Rich, Ph.D.

Loving Healing Press is pleased to an-
nounce Robert Rich, Ph.D. as Series Editor for the *10-Step Empowerment Series*.
This exciting new series conveys practical
guides written by seasoned therapists for
solving real-life problems.

Robert Rich, M.Sc., Ph.D., M.A.P.S.,
A.A.S.H. is a highly experienced counsel-
ing psychologist. His web site www.anxietyanddepression-
help.com is a storehouse of helpful information for people
suffering from anxiety and depression.

Bob is also a multiple award-winning writer of both fic-
tion and non-fiction, and a professional editor. His writing
is displayed at www.bobswriting.com. You are advised not
to visit him there unless you have the time to get lost for a
while.

Three of his books are tools for psychological self-help:
*Anger and Anxiety: Be in charge of your emotions and con-
trol phobias, Personally Speaking: Single session email
therapy,* and *Cancer: A personal challenge.* However, his
philosophy and psychological knowledge come through in
all his writing, which is perhaps why three of his books
have won international awards, and he has won many
minor prizes. Dr. Rich currently resides at Wombat Hollow
in Australia.

Bibliography

Bradshaw, J. (1992). *Homecoming: Reclaiming and championing your inner child.* New York, NY: Bantam Books.

Ford, D. (1999). *The dark side of the light chasers.* New York, NY: Riverhead Trade.

Lerner, H. G. (1990). *The dance of intimacy.* New York, NY: Perennial Library.

Newman, M. & Berkowitz, B. (1993). *How to be your own best friend.* New York, NY: Ballantine Books.

Peck, M. S. (1978). *The road less traveled.* New York, NY: Touchstone.

Siegel, D .J. & Hartzell, M. (2003). *Parenting from the inside out.* New York, NY: Penguin Group.

Shapiro, F. (1995). *Eye movement desensitization and reprocessing: Basic principles. protocols, and procedures.* New York, NY: The Guilford Press.

Stone, H. & Stone, S. (1989). Embracing ourselves. Novato, CA: New World Library.

Tolle, E. (1999). The power of now. Novato, CA: New World Library.

Van der Kolk, B. A., McFarlane, A. C., & Weisaeth, L. (1996). *Traumatic stress.* New York, NY: The Guilford Press.

Index

FREE BONUS GIFT

Do you find that your life is on hold or stuck in the same old pattern? Do you feel like you are constantly spinning your wheels but not getting the results you want? Are you clueless as to what to do to make your life better?

To help you gain an even greater sense of choice, Dr. Karen at **www.ChoiceRelationships.com** is offering you a bonus:

To claim it, go to:
www.ChoiceRelationships/artofchoicebonus

Printed in the United States
140709LV00003B/77/P